D1662673

MAXIM IVANOV

Painting and Graphic Art

Malerei und Graphik

PALACE EDITIONS

BIOGRAPHY

1975	Born in Kostroma
1986–1990	Studied at art school in Leningrad
1990–1992	Studied at the art college of the Vera Mukhina State Academy of Art and Design, St Petersburg
1993–1995	Attended painting and drawing classes at the Vera Mukhina State Academy of Art and Design, St Petersburg
From 1995	Student of the Vera Mukhina Academy, department of graphic design

Contributes to various exhibitions

BIOGRAPHIE

1975	In der Stadt Kostroma geboren.
1986–1990	Studium an der Kunstschule in Leningrad.
1990–1992	Studium an der Kunstschule Sankt-Petersburg Staatlich, Kunstgewerbeakademie namens V. P. Muchina.
1993–1995	studierte Zeichnung und Malerei an der Sankt-Petersburger Staatlichen Kunstgewerbeakademie namens V. P. Muchina.
seit 1995	Studium an der Sankt-Petersburger Staatlichen Kunstgewerbeakademie namens V. P. Muchina, Fakultät für Graphikdesign.

Ausstellungsbeteiligungen.

Maxim Ivanov is an artist so young that the attention of a critic who has seen much in his lifetime requires special explanation. I shall therefore explain. In modern art, as in the art of all other times, there is no shortage of young people. The majority of them, however, interpret youth as a strategy. Take a beginning Action artist for example. He must embody youthful aggression, radicalism and attack the former leaders of the pack, snarling at them and soiling their canvases with his spray. The angry young man splashes in all directions. The Conceptualist, on the other hand, by definition the quietest and most thoughtful, selects the strategy of a lay brother or loyal disciple and much is forgiven.

In short, it is not easy to be young. Especially, in the words of the Soviet cult film, when youth is the means of providing for one's old age.

Incidentally, it never was easy to be young, not even in the days of Soviet officiose, when youth art was an entire industry. Back then, the concept of a young artist was institutionalized with state firmness, without fools. The bearer of this title thoroughly understood his manoeuvre. One was supposed to respect one's elders, whilst not duplicating their thickness, flesh and fame. Hence the flagged zone of admissible youth, thematicized subjectly and, so as to say, optically; by a mixing of the colour spectrum in the direction of brightness and plastics towards spirited vigour. One might say, blessed is he who was young in his youth. For as the years go by, he is able to endure the cold of officiose. It is no surprise, therefore, that just as the former Komsomol activists made the best marketeers, so too did the shrewdest purveyors of the commercial galleries come out of the professionals of the youth associations. But enough about this. Conduct in art is a problem common to all strategists of youth. They quickly grow old. Old and out of date.

It is nice to see when an artist at the outset of his career is simply young. Without any introspections about it. Or strategies. Like Voltaire's Candide.

Ivanov is considered to be one such artist. He has a young appetite. Young teeth. A young eye. And all directed on art. In the given case, in the context of this exhibition, it is directed on the geometric tradition. Ivanov tries it out on his teeth, his taste, his eye. And it has to be said that he has a good eye. His work at the Russian Museum's department of modern art tells here. An eye that Leskov would call adjusted. Adjusted to the geometrical project in all its manifestations – from orthodox, disciplined, disciplining and Malevich to internally unfettered and impulsive, as in Art Informel.

Ivanov is getting his young teeth into this area of culture. He still has no partialities or prejudices; he does not gravitate towards discipline or deconstruction. He has an appetite. He is awfully fond of how others did it and no less keen to do it himself. Like a teenager allowed to go for a spin in a new car – this is the only way he can learn to drive and pave his own way. If, however, the teenager's skills are part of a concrete biography, then the joy of independent travel, an obedient steering wheel and the whistle of the wind in the hair can grow into an aesthetic quality in art. Ivanov achieves this quality. His geometric compositions are interesting, yet not in the transubstantiation of the impulses of the great masters of the geometric project (they can be read lightly, yet the essence does not lie in this reading). Nor in the transubstantiation of impulses from life, though they, be they a house, chair or fence, are jauntily rhythmicized and take the form of visual shorthand, surrendering completely to deciphering.

They are interesting for their young, frank and ingenuous appetite for form. This appetite rips through the typological proximity of the compositions, shaking up the rapport and chewing through the serious. Every device is aimed at quenching visual thirst, especially sharply felt in the era of the strategies of mediation, simulation and relativity. And as long as visual thirst exists, young art will obey its thirst.

Alexander Borovsky

Daß ein erfahrener Kritiker von einem so jungen Künstler wie Maxim Ivanov schreibt, muß extra erklärt werden. Ich erkläre. In der zeitgenössischen Kunst gibt es, wie auch in allen Zeiten, genug junge Künstler. Aber die meisten von ihnen verstehen ihre Jugend als eine bestimmte Strategie. Wenn man zum Beispiel ein junger Aktionskünstler ist, muß man junge Aggression und Radikalismus artikulieren, frühere Leittiere angreifen, sie anknurren oder ihre Leinwände mit Farbspray besprühen. Wenn man ein "Neuer Wilder" ist, muß man das aus Leibeskräften tun, mit viel Spritzer ringsherum. Wenn man ein Konzeptkünstler, das heißt, ein stiller und zum Nachdenken geneigter Mensch ist, so muß man die Strategie eines Klosterschülers, eines treuen Adepten wählen, – vieles wird dir verziehen.

Es ist also schwer, jung zu sein. Besonders, wenn die Jugend, wie es in einem sowjetischen Kultfilm heißt, das Mittel ist, den Lebensabend zu versorgen.

Zwar war es schon immer schwer, jung zu sein, sogar in der sowjetischen offiziösen Kunst, als die junge Kunst eine Industrie war. Damals wurde der Begriff "junger Künstler" staatlich und konkret institutionalisiert, ohne Possen zu reißen: der Träger dieses Titels verstand sein Manöver in allen Einzelheiten – es gehörte sich, Ältere zu verehren, ohne ihre Stämmigkeit, Fleischigkeit und Ehrwürdigkeit nachzuahmen. Deshalb gab es eine verlappte Zone der erlaubten Jugendlichkeit, welche sujetmäßig und sozusagen optisch – durch eine bestimmte Verschiebung zur Grellheit im Farbspektrum – und plastisch – durch die burschikose schwungvolle Manier – thematisiert wurde. Sozusagen, selig ist, der in seinen Jugendjahren jung war. Der hat ja die Kälte der offiziösen Kunst glücklich überstanden. Kein Wunder, daß professionelle Mitglieder der Vereinigungen junger Künstler zu den schlauesten Lieferanten kommerzieller Galerien geworden sind – genau so wie die besten Marktfunktionäre aus Komsomolaktivisten ausgeschlüpft sind. Aber genug davon – alle, die ihre Jugend als eine Benehmensstrategie in der Kunst begreifen, haben eines gemeinsam: Sie werden schnell alt. Sie veralten schnell.

Es ist sehr angenehm zu sehen, daß ein Künstler am Beginn seiner Art-Karriere einfach jung ist. Ohne jedwede Reflexion darüber. Ohne jedwede Strategie. So ein Candide.

Ich glaube, Ivanov ist so einer. Er hat jungen Appetit. Junge Zähne. Junges Auge. Und alles für die Kunst. In diesem Fall, im Kontext dieser Ausstellung – für die geometrische Tradition. Ivanov kostet sie mit Zähnen und Augen. Apropos, er hat ein gutes Auge – infolge der Arbeit in der Abteilung der neusten Kunstströmungen des Staatlichen Russischen Museums. Sein Auge hat sich, wie Leskov einst gesagt hat, eingeschossen. Auf das geometrische Projekt in allen seinen Erscheinungsformen eingeschossen, – von der disziplinierten und disziplinierenden, a lá Malevič, bis zur innerlich freien, spontanen, wie in der Art Informel, wie bei P. Soulage.

In diese Kulturschicht bricht Ivanov mit junger Energie ein. Er hat noch keine Voreingenommenheiten und Vorurteile, keine Neigung zur Diszipliniertheit und De-konstruktion. Er hat Appetit. Es gefällt ihm sehr, wie die anderen das gemacht haben, und nicht weniger will er das selbst machen. Wie ein Teenager, dem es erlaubt ist, einen komplizierten Wagen zu fahren. Nur auf solche Weise kann ein Teenager fahren und auch seinen eigenen Weg finden lernen. Aber bei einem Teenager sind das einfach Meilensteine seiner konkreten Biographie, in der Kunst aber kann dieser Spaß am selbständigen Fahren, gehorsamen Lenken, Windpfeifen in den Ohren zur ästhetischen Qualität werden. Und Ivanov erreicht diese Qualität: Seine geometrischen Komposi-tionen sind nicht durch die Verarbeitung der von alten Meistern des geometrischen Projektes erhaltenen Anstöße interessant – diese Anstöße sind offensichtlich, aber darum geht es nicht. Und nicht durch die Verarbeitung der von der Natur erhaltenen Anstöße, obwohl auch sie, seien es flott rhythmisierte und visuell stenographierte Haus, Stuhl oder Staketenzaun, leicht dechiffriert werden können.

Maxim Ivanovs Kompositionen sind durch den jungen, unverhüllten und offen-herzigen Appetit zur Formgebung interessant. Dieser Appetit bricht durch die typo-logische Ähnlichkeit der Kompositionen durch, rüttelt Rapporte, lockert Serien-mäßigkeit. Jeder Kunstgriff hat die Stillung des visuellen Hungers zum Ziel, welcher in der Epoche der Vermittlungs-, Simulations- und Relativierungsstrategien besonders spürbar ist. Und solange dieser visuelle Hunger da ist, läßt sich die junge Kunst nicht verdorren.

Aleksandr Borovskij

1
Alien Voices
Oil on orgalite
140 x 120

Fremde Stimmen
Öl auf Hartfaserplatte
140 x 120

2
Postface
Tempera on orgalite
120 x 125

Nachwort
Tempera auf Hartfaserplatte
120 x 125

3
Dialogue
Oil on orgalite
130 x 120

Dialog
Öl auf Hartfaserplatte
130 x 120

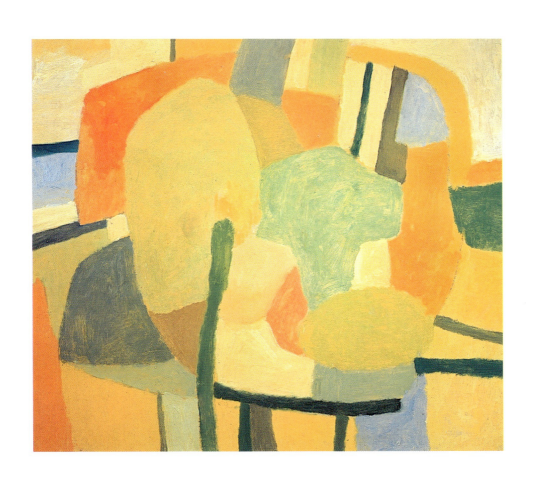

4
Broken Life
Tempera on orgalite
118 x 120

Gebrochenes Leben
Tempera auf Hartfaserplatte
118 x 120

5
Sorrow
Tempera on orgalite
120 x 130

Trauer
Tempera auf Hartfaserplatte
120 x 130

6
Labyrinth
Tempera on orgalite
123 x 120

Labyrinth
Tempera auf Hartfaserplatte
123 x 120

7
Dead Season
Tempera on orgalite
120 x 120

Sauregurkenzeit
Tempera auf Hartfaserplatte
120x120

8
Street
Tempera on orgalite
115 x 120

Straße
Tempera auf Hartfaserplatte
115x120

9
In Port
Tempera on orgalite
120 x 124

Im Hafen
Tempera auf Hartfaserplatte
120 x 124

10
Midday
Tempera on orgalite
120 x 130

Mittag
Tempera auf Hartfaserplatte
120 x 130

11
Japanese Garden
Tempera on orgalite
130 x 120

Japanischer Garten
Tempera auf Hartfaserplatte
130 x 120

12

Winter Landscape (1)

Gouache on paper

57 x 80

Winterlandschaft (1)

Gouache auf Papier

57 x 80

13
Winter Landscape (2)
Gouache on paper
54 x 75

Winterlandschaft (2)
Gouache auf Papier
54 x 75

14
- 21 C
Oil on canvas
95 x 95

- 21° C
Öl auf Leinwand
95 x 95

15
Winter Sun
Oil on canvas
95 x 95

Wintersonne
Öl auf Leinwand
95 x 95

16
Aggression
Gouache on paper
47 x 66

Aggression
Gouache auf Papier
47 x 66

17
Old Courtyard
Tempera on orgalite
120 x 130

Alter Hof
Tempera auf Hartfaserplatte
120 x 130

18
In January
Tempera on orgalite
120 x 135

Im Januar
Tempera auf Hartfaserplatte
120 x 135

19
Empty House
Tempera on orgalite
120 x 135

Leeres Haus
Tempera auf Hartfaserplatte
120 x 135

20
Situation
Tempera on orgalite
120 x 130

Situation
Tempera auf Hartfaserplatte
120 x 130

21
Game
Mixed media
100 x 100

Spiel
Mischtechnik
100 x 100

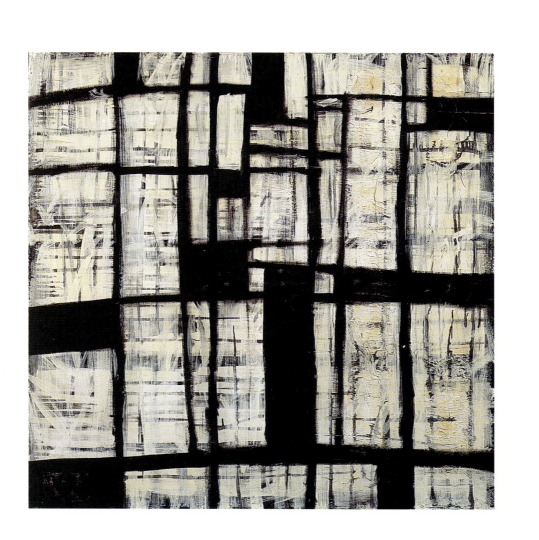

22
Reflection
Oil on orgalite
120 x 135

Widerspiegelungen
Öl auf Hartfaserplatte
120 x 135

23
Window Opposite
Tempera on orgalite
120 x 115

Fenster gegenüber
Tempera auf Hartfaserplatte
120 x 115

24
Promise
Tempera on orgalite
115 x 115

Versprechung
Tempera auf Hartfaserplatte
115 x 115

25
Glance out a Window
Tempera on orgalite
120 x 115

Blick aus dem Fenster
Tempera auf Hartfaserplatte
120 x 115

26
Recollection
Tempera on orgalite
117 x 117

Erinnerung
Tempera auf Hartfaserplatte
117 x 117

27
Corner of Vision
Tempera on orgalite
115 x 115

Sehwinkel
Tempera auf Hartfaserplatte
115 x 115

28
House on the Outskirts
Gouache on paper
47 x 67

Haus am Standrand
Gouache auf Papier
47 x 67

29
Seventh Floor
Gouache on paper
45 x 65

Das siebte Stockwerk
Gouache auf Papier
45 x 65

30
Different Life
Tempera on orgalite
115 x 120

Ein anderes Leben
Tempera auf Hartfaserplatte
115 x 120

31
Bed
Tempera on orgalite
116 x 120

Bett
Tempera auf Hartfaserplatte
116 x 120

32
Children's Games 2
Oil on canvas
95 x 95

Kinderspiele 2
Öl auf Leinwand
95 x 95

33
Children's Games 1
Oil on canvas
95 x 95

Kinderspiele 1
Öl auf Leinwand
95 x 95

34
Rush Hour
Tempera on orgalite
120 x 130

Spitzenzeit
Tempera auf Hartfaserplatte
120x130

35
Housing Scheme
Oil on canvas
95 x 95

Neubau
Öl auf Leinwand
95x95

36
Door
Oil on canvas
95 x 95

Tür
Öl auf Leinwand
95 x 95

37
Back Staircase
Oil on canvas
95 x 95

Hintertreppe
Öl auf Leinwand
95x95

38
Pendulum
Oil on canvas
95 x 95

Pendel
Öl auf Leinwand
95 x 95

39
Wall 2
Oil on canvas
95 x 95

Mauer 2
Öl auf Leinwand
95 x 95

40
Line of Horizon 3
Gouache on paper
41 x 66

Horizontlinie 3
Gouache auf Papier
41 x 66

Publisher
Herausgeber
Joseph Kiblitsky

Photography
Vassily Vorontsov

© 1999, PALACE EDITIONS
ISBN 3-930775-68-9 (Germany)

Printed in Italy by GRAFICART - Formia (LT)
Bookbindery: Salvatore Tonti (Napoli) Italy

Front cover:
Extinguishing Hesitations 2
Oil on canvas. 95 x 95

Umschlagvorderseite:
Abklingende Schwingungen 2
Öl auf Leinwand. 95 x 95

Back cover:
Line of Horizon 2
Oil on canvas. 95 x 95

Umschlagrückseite:
Horizontlinie 2
Öl auf Leinwand. 95 x 95

All works since 1998

Alle Arbeiten sind aus 1998